Dear Parents:

Congratulations! Your child is taking the first steps on an exciting journey. The destination? Independent reading!

STEP INTO READING® will help your child get there. The program offers five steps to reading success. Each step includes fun stories and colorful art or photographs. In addition to original fiction and books with favorite characters, there are Step into Reading Non-Fiction Readers, Phonics Readers and Boxed Sets, Sticker Readers, and Comic Readers—a complete literacy program with something to interest every child.

Learning to Read, Step by Step!

Ready to Read   Preschool–Kindergarten
• big type and easy words • rhyme and rhythm • picture clues
For children who know the alphabet and are eager to begin reading.

Reading with Help   Preschool–Grade 1
• basic vocabulary • short sentences • simple stories
For children who recognize familiar words and sound out new words with help.

Reading on Your Own   Grades 1–3
• engaging characters • easy-to-follow plots • popular topics
For children who are ready to read on their own.

Reading Paragraphs   Grades 2–3
• challenging vocabulary • short paragraphs • exciting stories
For newly independent readers who read simple sentences with confidence.

Ready for Chapters   Grades 2–4
• chapters • longer paragraphs • full-color art
For children who want to take the plunge into chapter books but still like colorful pictures.

STEP INTO READING® is designed to give every child a successful reading experience. The grade levels are only guides; children will progress through the steps at their own speed, developing confidence in their reading.

Remember, a lifetime love of reading starts with a single step!

With thanks to Charles M. Yurgalevitch, PhD, Director, School of Professional Horticulture, The New York Botanical Garden, for his help in the preparation of this book.

Visit us on the Web!
Seussville.com
StepIntoReading.com
rhcbooks.com

Educators and librarians, for a variety of teaching tools, visit us at RHTeachersLibrarians.com

Library of Congress Cataloging-in-Publication Data is available upon request.
ISBN 978-0-593-30616-1 (trade) — ISBN 978-0-593-30617-8 (lib. bdg.)

Printed in the United States of America
10 9 8 7 6 5 4 3 2 1

STEP INTO READING®

STEP 2

READING WITH HELP

A SCIENCE READER

Would You, Could You Plant a Tree?

With Dr. Seuss's Lorax

by Todd Tarpley

illustrated by Patrick Spaziante

Random House 🏠 New York

4

I am the Lorax.

I speak for the trees!

The trees need our help.

Can you help the trees, please?

Smoke from some factories
goes in the air.
Up, up, up, up!
There is smoke everywhere!

The smoke makes us cough.

The smoke makes us wheeze.

Too many factories.

Not enough trees!

Trees are quite useful.
They help clean the air.
They help remove lots of
the bad things found there.

Many creatures—like birds—
make their home in the trees.
Chipmunks and squirrels,
even insects like bees!

Trees also make shade,

which helps lower heat.

And many trees grow

the good food that we eat!

How can YOU help the trees?
I am glad that you asked!
For that is exactly
our very next task.

We will plant a new tree.

We will have lots of fun!

In fact, we may even

plant more trees than one!

Do you live in a place
that is sunny and hot?

Or a place that is cloudy
and rainy a lot?

Trees have different needs
for soil, water, and sun.
You have to be careful
to plant the right one.

A wide-spreading oak?

Well, it may grow just fine . . .

in a place that would never

be right for a pine.

A palm tree might thrive
in the hot and dry air.

20

But an evergreen tree?

It may not like it there.

This big-rooted cypress
grows where it is wetter.

Acacias, however,
like deserts much better.

Which kind will you choose?

There are thousands of trees!

Some trees are so tall

that they sway in the breeze.

Some trees are so small

that they don't reach your knees.

Have you ever seen trees

that are stranger than these?

Once you find the right type,
you are ready to go.
Choose a spot in the sun
where you want it to grow.

You might want to plant
a seed, acorn, or berry.
And you may grow a tree.
(Is this fast? No, not very!)

But here is a plan
that you may try instead.
It will help you start faster—
move full speed ahead!

At a place called a nursery,
tree experts grow trees.
They come in small pots
and are sold, just like these.

Then take your tree home,
and plant it with care.
And when you are done?
What a tree you have there!

It takes many years
for a tree to grow tall—
just like a person,
who starts very small.

But once it grows bigger,
then, oh, what a thrill—
it will help clean the air!
Yes, I promise! It will!

If each of us—EACH OF US—
plants JUST ONE TREE,
just think what a wonderful
world this will be!